D0848662

THE ADVENTURES
& BRAVE DEEDS of

THE SHIP'S CAT

ON THE SPANISH MAINE

TOGETHER WITH
THE MOST LAMENTABLE
LOSSE OF THE

ALCESTIS

& Triumphant Firing of the Port of
CHAGRES

Truthfully Narrated in Verses by
MR. RICHARD ADAMS

AND IN DIVERS CUNNING AND
FANTASTICAL PICTURES BY
MR. ALAN ALDRIDGE
with MR. Harry Willock

Emprinted for Her Majestie's Loyall Subjects by
Master Jonathan Cape at Thirty Bedford Square in London,
in the Yeare of Our Lorde MCMLXXVII

to
Rosamond & Juliet
Miles, Saffron, Pim & Marc
Stephen & David

First Published 1977
Reprinted 1979

Jonathan Cape Ltd,
30 Bedford Square, London WC1

British Library Cataloguing in Publication Data

Adams, Richard, b. 1920
The ship's cat.
I. Title AI. Aldridge, Alan
821'.9'14 PR6051.D345

ISBN *0-224-01441-2*

Printed in Italy by New Interlitho SpA

"It chanced by fortune that the shippes cat leapt into the sea, which being downe, kept her selfe very valiantly above water, notwithstanding the great waves, still swimming, the which the Master knowing, he caused the skiffe with half a dozen men to goe towards her and fetch her again, when she was almost halfe a mile from the shippe, and all this while the shippe lay on staies. I hardly believe they would have made such haste and meanes if one of our company had been in like peril."

Hakluyt

I

Ahoy! The old Alcestis,
The Spaniards' bane and death,
That sails the thirteenth parallel
Before the trade winds' breath.
And here's an English cat, by heck!
To serve unmoved through fire and wreck,
To climb the yards and swab the deck
For Queen Elizabeth.

II

The billows roll, the wind blows fair
The lofty sails to fill:
And westward ho! For Providence
They sail her with a will.
And in the rigging day by day
The cat's awatch for Spanish prey,
Some merchant bound for Cadiz bay
Or plate ship for Seville.

III

Captain, I see a Spanish ship
Upon the starboard quarter,
And she's alone!" "Ho! Clear the decks!
We'll bring the Dons to slaughter!"
But in an hour there came nine more.
"I'd fight with three, or even four,
But here's a fleet of half a score.
They'll blow us from the water!"

IV

The ship's cat, standing to his gun,
Observes the Spanish sail.
The Master Gunner grins and shrugs
And tweaks him by the tail.
"I doubt we cannot fight the lot.
I doubt the knocks will be too hot,
But better sink than lie and rot
In some foul Cadiz gaol."

V

Alas! Alas! Alcestis,
Surrounded and outgunned!
Two Spanish ships have grappled her
And eight more lie beyond.
The ship's cat, swearing in the smoke,
Fought till his blunted halberd broke,
Before a heavy cutlass stroke
Stretched him inert and stunned.

VI

What boots to sharpen English claws,
What boots to spit and mew,
Shackled below the Spanish decks
With thirty of the crew?
To lie and hear the bilboes clink,
To smell the bilge and prison stink,
Weevils to munch and scum to drink,
What weary days ensue!

VII

At last the Spanish fleet makes port,
The anchors clatter down.
The wretched English prisoners
Are marched through Chagres town:
Brought to the market-place, before
Don Esteban, the Governor,
To taste the bitter luck of war
Against the Spanish crown.

VIII

The Governor's escort rapped the Master
Gunner on the head.
"We see there's thirty cowards alive,
How many more are dead?"
The ship's cat, spitting with disgrace,
Leapt for his throat and tore his lace
And clawed him in his swarthy face
Until the rascal bled.

IX

"Come, take these English pirates,"
Don Esteban did say,
"And fling them into Chagres gaol
Without an hour's delay!
And give that cat a ball and chain,
For in this town he shall remain
To serve the priests and Dons of Spain
Until his dying day.

X

This is some lewd familiar
That's served an English witch.
Send for the Inquisition
To make his whiskers twitch!
Here, gaoler's daughter, guard him well,
And lock him in the darkest cell,
An heretick, an infidel,
A soul as black as pitch!"

XI

Alone, he lifted up his voice
All in the tropic night.
"Greensleeves was all my joy," he sang,
"Greensleeves was my delight."
Her tender heart was moved with pity
To hear the luckless English kitty
A-singing of his plaintive ditty
Without or fire or light.

XII

"Pray, Father, give that honest cat
Some straw to make a bed,
And let me bring him meat and drink
And wash his broken head.
And when he's mended he'll be able
To catch the ratten in the stable,
To mind the house and wait at table,"
The gaoler's daughter said.

DB
HW

XIII

They've dressed him in a leather smock
And taught him how to pour
The gaoler's wine and how to tend
The lamps and sweep the floor.
The dismal gaoler works him hard
And when he goes into the yard
A Spanish cat is put on guard
And watches from the door.

XIV

On Philip's day the gaoler's mates
Sat drinking half the night.
"Now, English cat, fetch up more wine
And bring another light.
And do it quick!" the gaoler roared,
"As quick as when you dropped your sword
The day the Spaniards came aboard
To teach you how to fight!"

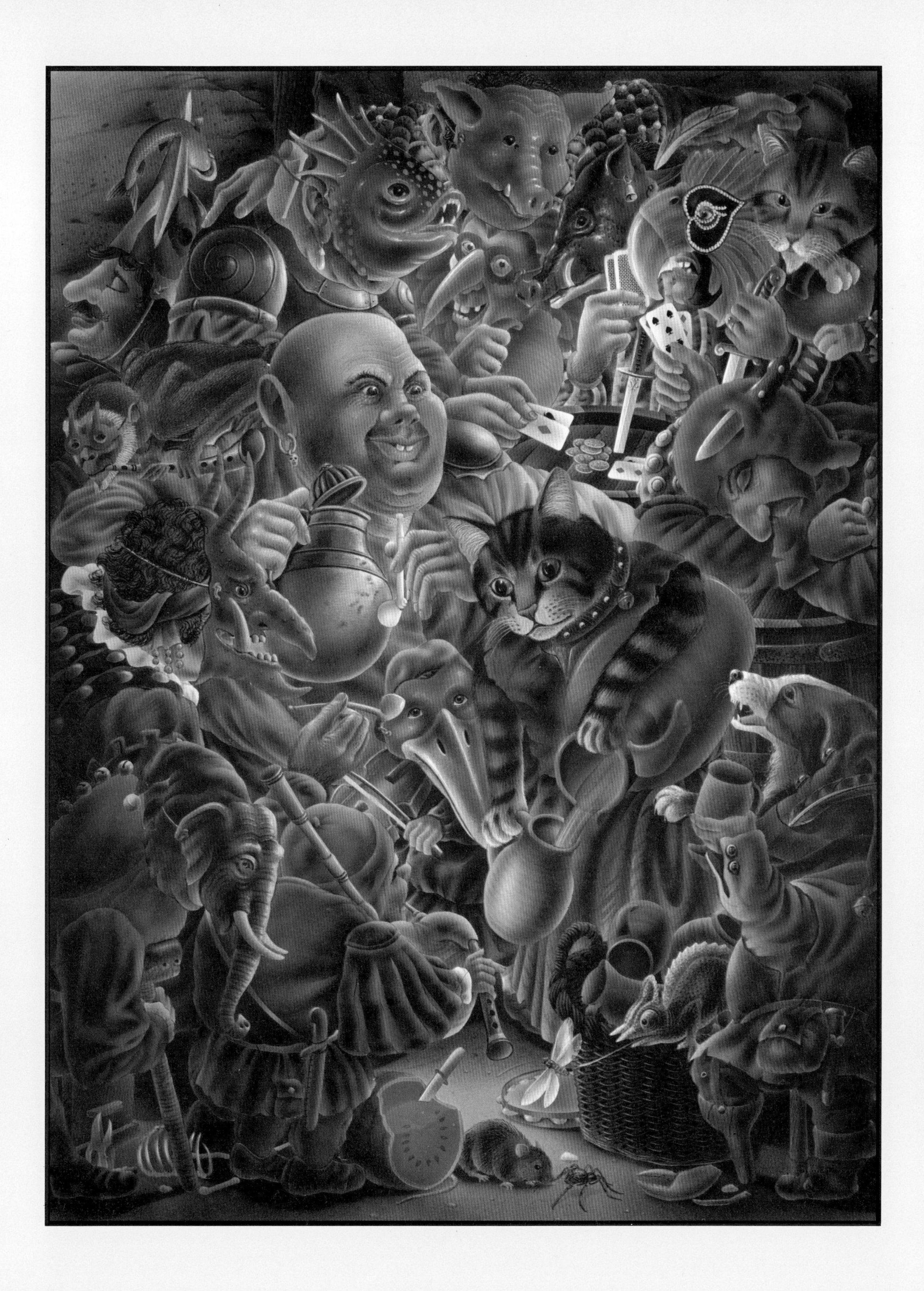

XV

At last the drunken fellows slept,
Their heads upon their knees,
And from the loosened leather belt
He slips the bunch of keys.
Outside he met the Spanish cat
And knocked him down and beat him flat
And left his body on the mat
As tidy as you please.

XVI

Then quickly, quickly to the gaol
And open wide the door.
The desperate crew came pouring out
With one tremendous roar:
"Hurrah for English bravery!
No popery, no slavery,
No Jesuitical knavery!
We'll pay the landlord's score!"

XVII

Make haste," the Master Gunner cried,
"Yarely, good fellows, skip!
Run to the harbour, fire the dock
And seize the likeliest ship.
No wind, and we must do without.
Take to the boats and tow her out!
Cat, swing the lead and sound about!
We'll give the Dons the slip."

XVIII

A half-mile out, they caught the breeze
As dawn began to pale.
The ship's cat, searching, found a glass,
And laid it on the rail.
And as he watched the harbour burn
First once, then twice, he could discern
A Spanish pinnace, full astern,
Approaching under sail.

XIX

Good Master Gunner, use your skill,
The Dons are in pursuit!
Say, shall we turn her broadside on
And show them how to shoot?"
"Alas, good cat, the powder's wet.
I fear the Dons will take us yet.
But come, we'll ram them! Ay, and let's
Lay on most resolute!"

XX

Then sunrise shows the tattered band
Two other ships come on.
"Master, those masts are Plymouth-rigged,
Or else my wits are gone!
Their guns are manned! How fast they near!"
"Fond, silly cat, and canst not cheer?
It's Frankie Drake, it's Drake is here!
The Pasha *and the* Swan*!"*

XXI

The Spanish pinnace sheered away,
The English ships drew near,
Amazed to hear a Spanish craft
That gave an English cheer.
But when young Drake had proved it true
That this half-starved and verminous few
Were all the old Alcestis' *crew,*
He could not hide a tear.

XXII

He gave them victuals, scant enough,
But all that he could spare,
And sent his carpenters aboard
To put them in repair.
And when they were securely found
He wished them joy of Plymouth Sound,
And for the Isthmus he is bound –
And then for anywhere.

XXIII

And where hast thou been, truant cat?"
"Watching the after-hold.
I would not trouble Master Drake
With that I can unfold."
"What then, good tib, we fain would know?"
"Then follow, friends. Come look below
And see the marvel I will show.
She's full of pearls and gold!"

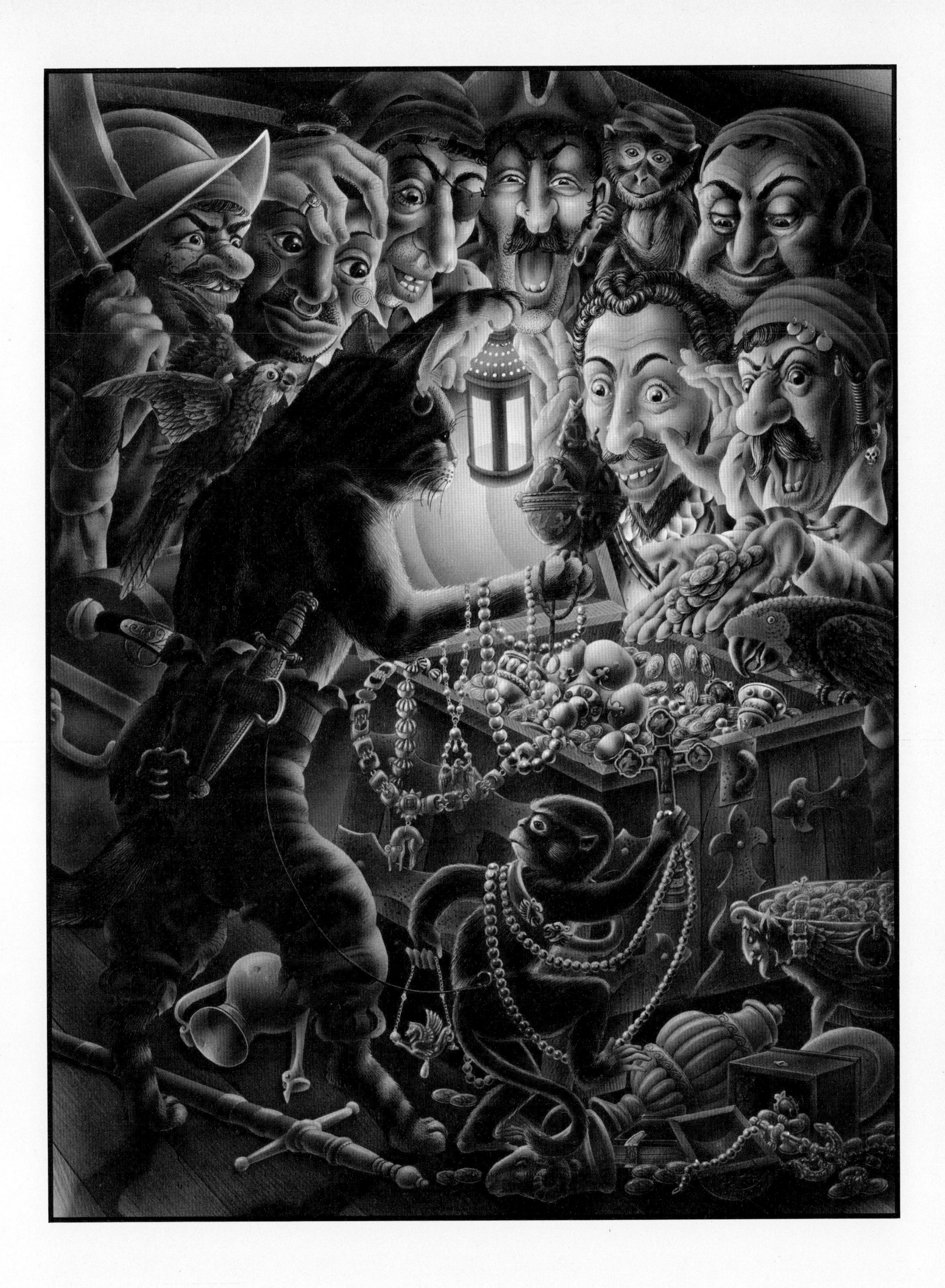

XXIV

O eastward ho! For Providence,
Across to the Azores!
And now they've sighted Ushant
And now the Devon shores.
And when they came to Plymouth strand
They sent a courier up the land
To bear the news to Cecil and
The Privy Councillors.

XXV

Our cat sent twenty sacks of pearls
And many a glistering bar,
Inscribed, "To Merrie England's Queene,
Fairer than any star."
Now see him, called to Richmond's halls,
As down upon one paw he falls.
She taps him with her sword and calls,
"Arise, Sir Tom de Chat!"

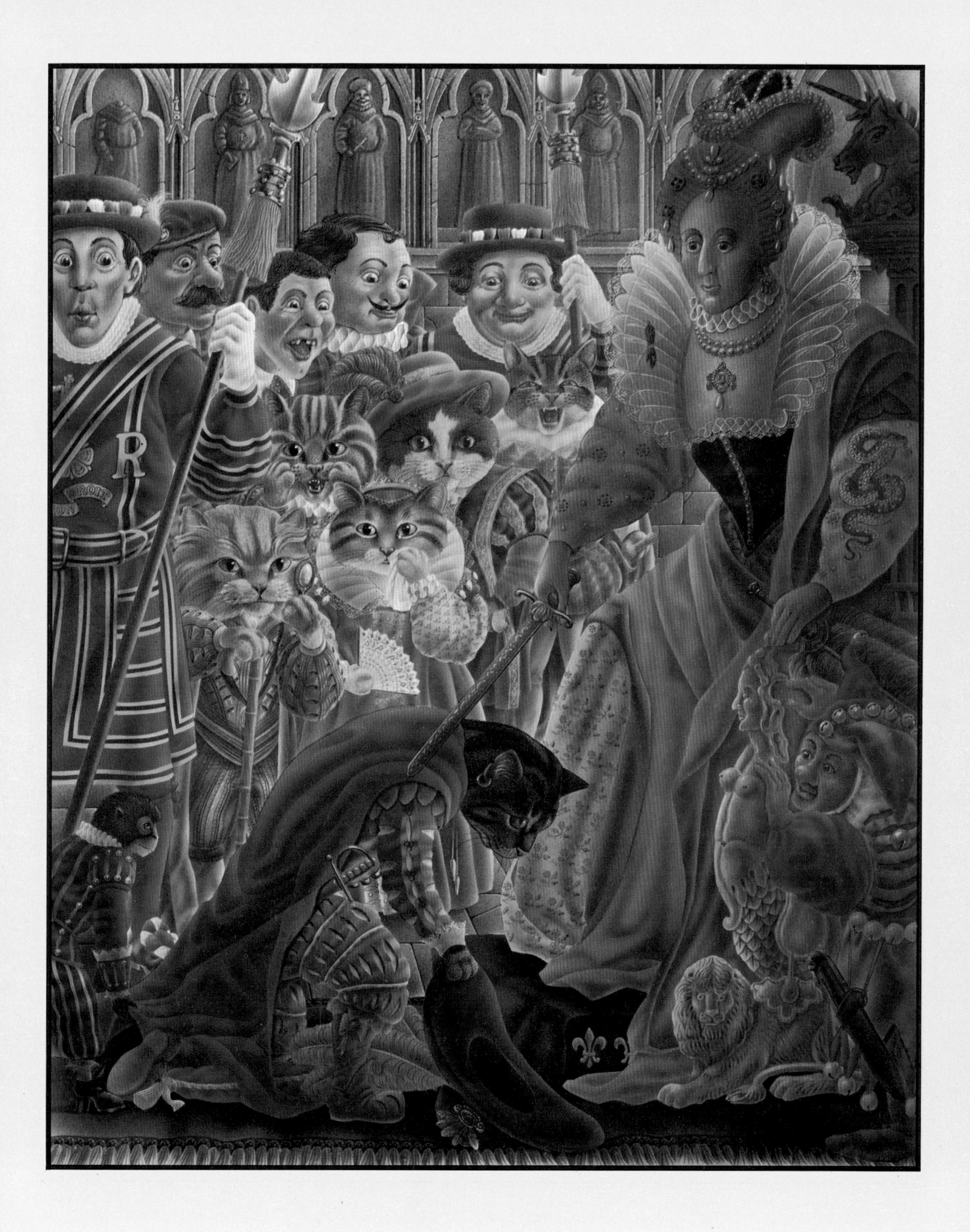

XXVI

All in the jocund Berkshire vale
Sir Tom lived out his days,
Father of many a swaggering kit,
As gentle Aubrey says.
May England have such fellows yet
That will not shrink their paws to wet
And let us see that none forget
(Good Rosamond and Juliet)
Their noble fame to praise.

THE END